CONTENTS

L B Books

Published 2024. Little Brother Books Ltd, Ground Floor, 23 Southernhay East, Exeter, Devon EX1 1QL
books@littlebrotherbooks.co.uk | www.littlebrotherbooks.co.uk
Printed in the United Kingdom.
The Little Brother Books trademark, email and website addresses, are the sole and exclusive properties of Little Brother Books Limited.

ONLINE ACTIVITIES

On some of the pages you will see QR codes. These QR codes take you to online Purple Mash activities which support learning from the relevant page.

To use the QR codes, scan the QR code with the camera on your web enabled tablet, click on the link and the activity will appear on screen.

Alternatively, QR readers are available on the app store for your device.

SCAN CODE

purple mash

NUMBERS TO 10,000,000

Wallace and Gromit's Top Bun bakery is in demand! They have so many orders, they have had to keep a log of how many grams they have of each ingredient.

1

Write down the value of the digits highlighted in **red**. The first one has been done for you.

M	HTh	TTh	Th	H	T	O	Value of red digit
Millions	Hundred Thousands	Ten Thousands	Thousands	Hundreds	Tens	Ones	
2	3	6	3	2	0	1	60,000
1	1	4	1	5	1	3	
5	6	0	8	7	9	7	
5	1	8	4	3	9	1	
3	1	0	7	0	1	5	
4	4	8	6	8	3	9	

2

Help Wallace and Gromit finish their recipes by writing down the written numbers in figures. The first one has been done for you.

a. Five million, six hundred and fifty five thousand, three hundred and forty five.

> 5,655,345

b. Nine million, eight hundred and eight thousand, three hundred and eleven.

c. Two million, four hundred and forty six thousand, six hundred and fifty one.

d. One million, seven hundred and twenty nine thousand and four.

e. Nine Million, nine hundred and nine thousand, nine hundred.

ROUNDING NUMBERS

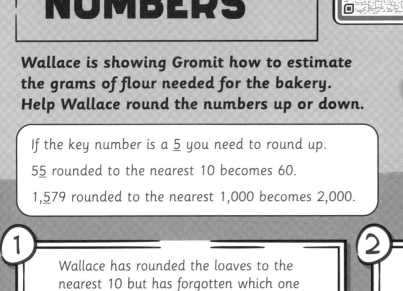

Wallace is showing Gromit how to estimate the grams of flour needed for the bakery. Help Wallace round the numbers up or down.

> If the key number is a <u>5</u> you need to round up.
>
> 5<u>5</u> rounded to the nearest 10 becomes 60.
>
> 1,<u>5</u>79 rounded to the nearest 1,000 becomes 2,000.

1

Wallace has rounded the loaves to the nearest 10 but has forgotten which one goes with which. Can you draw lines from the number to the nearest 10?

45	90
32	30
91	40
35	50
75	80

2

Draw a circle around all the numbers that, when rounded to the nearest hundred, will equal 300.

256   377

398

309   299

3

Draw a circle around all the numbers that, when rounded to the nearest thousand, will equal 8000.

8,888   8,808

8,008

8,080   8,401

4

Draw a circle around all the numbers that, when rounded to the nearest ten thousand, will equal 50,000.

49,356   56,651

45,001

59,090   48,743

5

a. The number 55 rounded to the nearest 10 is ☐ and to the nearest 100 is ☐.

b. The number 644 rounded to the nearest 100 is ☐ and to the nearest 1000 is ☐.

c. The number 7,369 rounded to the nearest 1,000 is ☐ and to the nearest 10,000 is ☐.

d. The number 73,009 rounded to the nearest 10,000 is ☐ and to the nearest 100,000 is ☐.

PROBLEM SOLVING

At the Wash 'n' Go window cleaning service, Wallace has been doing his accounts and learning all about big numbers. Gromit is helping by drawing his own place value grid and adding counters.

1

M	HTh	TTh	Th	H	T	O
Millions	Hundred Thousands	Ten Thousands	Thousands	Hundreds	Tens	Ones

a. What number has he created?

b. He adds 3 counters to the 'Tens' column. What is his new number?

c. He removes the 3 counters from the 'Tens' column and adds them to the 'Hundred Thousands' column. What is his new number?

d. He removes the 3 counters from the 'Hundred Thousands' column and adds them to the 'Ones' column. What is his new number?

2

At West Wallaby Street, Wallace has written the digits from Gromit's place value grid on number cards.

`1` `2` `5` `2` `8` `6` `9`

a. Use all the digits to create the highest number possible.

b. Use all the digits to create the lowest number possible.

c. Wallace makes a new number with the digit cards and gives Gromit some clues to guess what it is. Can you help Gromit work out what Wallace's number could be? Write down all the possibilities.

> The number has 5 digits. The number is greater than 50,000.
> The number has 9 ones. The number has the same number of tens and thousands.
> The number is less than 80,000. The 1-digit card has not been used.

NEGATIVE NUMBERS

It's nearly Christmas and Wallace and Gromit are desperate to get all their gift shopping finished so they can go sledging! They can only go after 4pm once all their work is done. The best conditions for sledging are when the temperature is between -1°C and -4 °C.

1

The – sign at the start of these numbers make them negative numbers. Negative numbers are numbers that are less than zero.

Which of the days will be best for sledging at 4pm? Complete the table below.

	Temperature at midday	Change in temperature between midday and 4pm	4pm temperature	Best for sledging? ✔ or ✖
Monday	4°C	-8°C	(4 - 8 = -4) -4°C	
Tuesday	7°C	-6°C		
Wednesday	1°C	-3°C		
Thursday	-1°C	-1°C		
Friday	5°C	-8°C		
Saturday	6°C	-5°C		
Sunday	0°C	-5°C		

2

Using your knowledge of negative numbers, compare the number sentences by filling in the missing greater than (>), less than (<) or equal to (=) symbol. The first one has been done for you.

a. 4 – 8 = -4 | < | 5 – 7 = -2

b. -3 + 5 | | -4 + 6

c. -8 + 9 | | -3 + 2

d. 6 – 10 | | 4 – 5

e. 6 – 10 | | -11 + 7

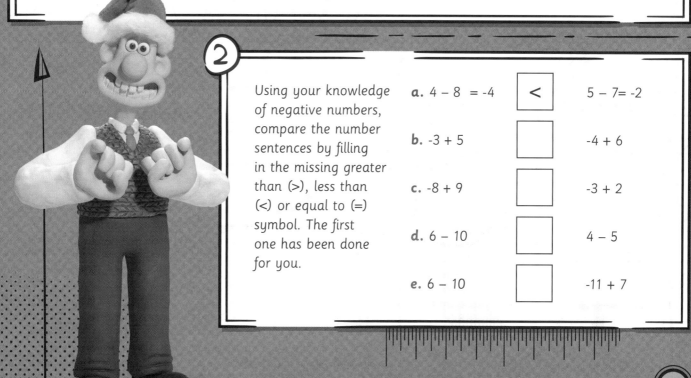

ROMAN NUMERALS

Wallace has been researching ideas for new inventions. He finds an ancient inventions book hidden in the back of a shop. Inside are pages filled with roman numerals. Each numeral has a different value.

I = 1, V = 5, X = 10, L = 50, C = 100, D = 500 and M = 1000.

These numerals can be joined together to make different values. When a smaller number is in front of a larger number, you subtract it, e.g., IV = 4 and XC = 90.

1

Put a tick next to the correct Roman numeral.

a. 80 =	XC	◯	LXXX	◯	XIV	◯	LXI	◯
b. 501 =	ID	◯	XC	◯	DI	◯	CXXXII	◯
c. 94 =	XCIV	◯	DIV	◯	MII	◯	LXX	◯
d. 990 =	CMXC	◯	MMC	◯	CVii	◯	CLXVI	◯
e. 18 =	VIII	◯	DL	◯	XV	◯	XVIII	◯

2

Fill in this table using numbers and Roman numerals.

a.	134	=		e.		=	DLXXI
b.	804	=		f.		=	XXIX
c.		=	DCCLXX	g.	554	=	
d.		=	CCCLXII	h.	880	=	

3

Put these years in order from earliest to latest.

MMXXII	MDCC	MCCLVI	MDCCCV	MCDXLI

ADDITION

Wallace and Gromit are testing their mechanical fishing rod reach. It can reach very far! They have recorded the distances every day this week, but which day did their rod reach the furthest?

The best way for Wallace and Gromit to work out their highest score is to add the two numbers together using the column method. When using this method, you start with the ones column and work to the left to the tens, hundreds then thousands column. When you add more than nine in one column, you 'carry' over the first digit to the column on its left.

If, one day, Wallace and Gromit recorded reaches of 2178m and 1356m, their overall score is 3534m.

Th	H	T	O
2	1	7	8
+ 1	3	5	6
3	5	3	4
		1	1

1

Help them work out their distances for each day.

a. Monday

```
    3 5 7 6
+ 2 3 1 2
_____
```

b. Tuesday

```
    7 3 8 4
+ 1 2 8 4
_____
```

c. Wednesday

```
    3 9 1 4
+     3 0 8
_____
```

d. Thursday

```
    4 5 6 7
+ 3 4 5 6
_____
```

e. Friday

```
    7 7 6 2
+ 1 0 2 8
_____
```

f. Saturday

```
    5 0 6 7
+     7 6 4
_____
```

g. Sunday

```
    5 3 4 5
+ 3 2 7 7
_____
```

2

Oh no! Wallace has accidentally spilt his cup of tea all over the distance sheets!

Can you help him work out the missing numbers?

a.

```
    4 ☐ 2 5
+ 2 6 3 6
_____
  6 9 6 1
        1
```

b.

```
    5 1 2 1
+ 2 ☐ 8 3
_____
  7 3 0 ☐
        1
```

c.

```
    4 4 5 8
+ 3 5 ☐ 8
_____
  ☐ 0 4 6
    1 1 1
```

SUBTRACTION

Wendolene has been selling balls of wool, but she's got into a real muddle. There are piles of wool everywhere. Can you help her work out how much wool she will have left after sending out her customer orders?

She had 9134 balls of wool to sell and successfully sold 1356 balls. How much wool does she have left to sell? To work this out, Wendolene can use the column method.

Remember, when you carry out subtraction with big numbers, you always start with the ones column and work to the left. If you do not have enough to subtract from in the ones column, you can 'borrow' from the tens column. If you do not have enough in the tens column, you can 'borrow' from the hundreds column, and so on. **9134 - 1356 = ?**

	Th	H	T	O
	$^8\cancel{9}$	$^{10}\cancel{1}$	$^{12}\cancel{3}$	$^{1}4$
-	1	3	5	6
	7	7	7	8

Wendolene has worked out she has 7778 balls of wool left. She needs to sell more next time!

1

Use the column method to work out the answers to these subtraction questions.

a.
```
    8 7 5 4
  - 2 3 1 1
  ─────────
```

b.
```
    6 5 3 9
  - 3 4 2 8
  ─────────
```

c.
```
    5 6 3 2
  -   7 6 3
  ─────────
```

d.
```
    9 6 3 8
  - 6 3 2 1
  ─────────
```

e.
```
    7 9 4 4
  - 6 4 3 8
  ─────────
```

f.
```
    8 5 3 3
  - 3 1 7 6
  ─────────
```

2

Wallace has helped Wendolene work out some of these questions. They have been comparing answers and their answers don't match! Which of the two has worked out the subtraction correctly? Circle the correct calculation for each question.

| Wallace | Wendolene |

a.
```
   Wallace              Wendolene
    5 11   1               1  1
   ⁵6̸ ¹¹2̸ ¹2̸ 1 5         6 2̸ 1 5
  -  3 8 3 3           -  3 8 3 3
  ─────────────        ─────────────
     2 3 8 2              3 9 8 2
```

b.
```
          3   1                      1
    7 5 4̸ 4̸              7 5 4 4
  - 2 4 1 9            - 2 4 1 9
  ─────────────        ─────────────
    5 1 2 5              5 1 3 5
```

c.
```
    1   1                    1   1   2
   2̸ 6 4 8              2̸ 6̸ 4̸ 8
  -   8 2 9            -   8 2 9
  ─────────────        ─────────────
    1 8 2 1              1 8 1 9
```

MENTAL ADDITION AND SUBTRACTION

Wallace has been trying to rewire the remote control for the techno-trousers to make them safe. It's not going very well, so far! He has written a list of statements about numbers to use to help him. Can you work out whether the statements are true or false?

1

Write **true** or **false** under each statement.

a. When an even number is added to an even number, the answer is always even.

b. When an odd number is added to an odd number, the answer is always odd.

c. When an odd number is added to an odd number, the answer is always even.

d. When you count forwards in 10s from 100, you will say the number 9800.

e. When you count backwards in 25s from 1000, you will say the number 175.

2

Wallace is saving up for a gadget. It costs £110, and he has already saved £61 in his piggy bank. To work out how much he still needs, he draws a simple bar diagram and works it out in his head.

> 110 - 60 is 50, then takeaway one more is 49.

110	
61	49

Wallace realises he still needs to save another £49.

Help him fill in the missing numbers on these bar diagrams.

a.

250	
121	

b.

342	
	132

c.

1559	
	1250

d.

161	
	41

e.

190	534

f.

703	227

MENTAL ADDITION AND SUBTRACTION

Wallace and Gromit's baking skills are in demand! They have so many orders to complete, but Gromit is missing some rolls from his orders. See if you can work out what's needed.

Wallace and Gromit are carrying trays filled with loaves and rolls.

Wallace is carrying 5 loaves and 25 rolls. Gromit is carrying 10 loaves. How many more rolls does Gromit need to add so there is the same number of items on his tray?

Wallace		Gromit
5 loaves + 25 rolls	=	10 loaves + 20 rolls

Gromit needs 20 more rolls to have the same quantity as Wallace.

1

Using mental strategies, fill in the missing numbers to make these number equations balance.

a. 60 + 30   =   40 + 50

b. 110 - 50   =   30 + ☐

c. 85 + ☐   =   120 - 15

d. 290 + ☐   =   160 + 245

e. 165 + 230   =   500 - ☐

f. 250 - ☐   =   -86 + 118

g. ☐ + 328   =   -500 - 160

h. 450 - 230   =   145 + ☐

i. 342 - 50   =   ☐ + 150

j. 20 + ☐   =   290 - 135

Look at this number pyramid. The numbers below always add up to the number above.

```
        470
    120     350
  20    100    250
```

For example:
20 + 100 = 120 and 120 - 100 = 20
100 + 250 = 350 and 350 - 100 = 250
120 + 350 = 470 and 470 - 120 = 350
This is why 470 is at the top of the pyramid.

2

Fill in the missing numbers on the number pyramids below.

a.
```
    330
      200
  60      130
```

b.
```
    600
      335
    250
```

c.
```
  95
    43   120
```

d.
```
  246
    136   170
```

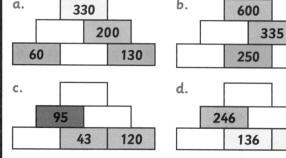

ADDITION AND SUBTRACTION

When solving multistep word problems, there will be more than one calculation that you need to do before finding your answer. Look at how Wendolene solved this problem below.

Wendolene is making a new window display to show off all of her lovely yarn colours. The red yarn is 129cm long, the yellow yarn is 150cm long and the pink yarn is 85cm longer than the yellow.

She needs all the pieces of yarn to be 120cm long. When she has cut them all to the correct length, how much yarn will she have left over in total?

Red yarn: 129 - 120 = 9cm left over.
Yellow yarn: 150 - 120 = 30cm left over.
Pink yarn: length (150 + 85) = 235cm. 235 - 120 = 115cm left over.
Total left over = 9 + 30 + 115 = 154cm of yarn.

1

Wallace is shopping for cheese. He has some vouchers that he got for his birthday - £50 from Gromit and £20 from a friendly neighbour – and he's saved £85.20 in his piggy bank. The cheese he wants to buy is £135. Can he afford it? How much money will he have left over?

2

Wallace and Gromit are going on a road trip. On the first day, Wallace drives him 130km. On the second day he drives double that. On the third day, he only drives 37km before Wallace realises the petrol light has come on! He began the journey on a full tank of petrol and normally the car can go 500km before he needs to fill up. The next petrol station is 15km away. Will he make it? How many km worth of petrol will he have to spare?

3

Wallace is measuring out the chemicals for his latest invention. In beaker **A** he adds 270ml of a red liquid and 323ml of a blue liquid. In beaker **B** he adds 180ml of a yellow liquid and 135ml of a green liquid. What is the difference in the amount of liquids in the two beakers?

4

Wallace has lots of inventions in progress! This week, he has worked a total of 1250 minutes. He worked for 235 minutes on the Jetpack, 380 minutes on the Tellyscope and 220 minutes on the Crackervac. He's spent the rest of the time working on the Autochef. How many minutes has he spent on the Autochef?

PRIME NUMBERS

Gromit is picking out boxes of bolts for Wallace. Can you help identify the boxes that have prime numbers of bolts in them?

A prime number is a number that is only divisible by one and itself, e.g., 13.

1

Circle all the boxes that have a prime number between 1 and 50.

2

Write all the prime numbers between the following numbers.

a. **50 – 59:**

b. **60 – 69:**

c. **70 – 79:**

d. **80 – 89:**

e. **90 – 99:**

3

Which two prime numbers between 0 and 20 have been added in each of these sums?

a. ☐ + ☐ = **8**   b. ☐ + ☐ = **28**

c. ☐ + ☐ = **15**   d. ☐ + ☐ = **21**

WRITTEN MULTIPLICATION

Gromit is a keen knitter. He can spend quite a time in Wendolene's shop, using multiplication to calculate how many balls of each colour she has in stock when planning his next project.

There are 4 boxes of bright red wool, each box holds 186 balls.

By multiplying the numbers, he has worked out there are 744 balls in total.

```
    H  T  O
    1  8  6
 x        4
 _____
    7  4  4
    3  2
```

1

Use your multiplication skills to work out the answers to these questions. Remember to start by multiplying the ones, then the tens and finally the hundreds. If you need to carry a number, write it underneath the next column.

Answer these questions using a written method.

a.
```
   H  T  O
   2  4  6
x        3
_____
```

b.
```
   H  T  O
   1  9  9
x        4
_____
```

c.
```
   H  T  O
   4  0  1
x        2
_____
```

d.
```
   H  T  O
   1  5  0
x        5
_____
```

e.
```
   H  T  O
   3  1  8
x        5
_____
```

f.
```
   H  T  O
   4  0  9
x        7
_____
```

g.
```
   H  T  O
   7  1  5
x        6
_____
```

h.
```
   H  T  O
   3  6  7
x        8
_____
```

2

Match the question to the correct answer. Use this space for your workings out.

a. 465 x 3 =   2055

b. 411 x 5 =   5496

c. 362 x 4 =   1395

d. 916 x 6 =   1448

WRITTEN MULTIPLICATION

Wallace wants to work out how much cheese the cheese shop has in stock. To work this out, he's counted that there are 48 blocks of 23 different flavours.

When multiplying a two-digit number by another two-digit number, you might wish to use the grid method. Fill in the missing numbers in the boxes and work out the answer by adding the numbers together. For example:

48 x 23 =

x	40	8	
20	800	160	960
3	120	24	+144
			1104

There are 1104 blocks of cheese in the store.

1

Complete these multiplication questions using the same method.

a.

24 x 19 =

x	20	4
10		
9		

b.

35 x 43 =

x	30	5
40		
3		

c.

36 x 25 =

x	30	6
20		
5		

d.

66 x 33 =

x	60	6
30		
3		

Another way to work out multiplication questions is to use the column method. Remember to put a 0 down when you multiply the tens. E.g.

```
        4 3
     x  2 3
43 x 3 = 1 2 9
43 x 20 = 8 6 0
        9 8 9
```

2

Use the column method to work out the answers to these questions.

a.
```
    3 4
  x 2 1
  _____
```

b.
```
    2 3
  x 2 2
  _____
```

c.
```
    3 4
  x 1 9
  _____
```

WRITTEN DIVISION

Wallace is baking pies. He needs 6 mushrooms per portion to make his vegetable pie and he has 453 mushrooms in the fridge. Wallace uses the formal written method of division to work out how many portions of pie he can make.

When doing written division, you always begin on the left. For each column, if there are any remainders, they are 'carried over' to the next column.

$$453 \div 6 \text{ is written as} \quad 6 \begin{array}{|cccc} 0 & 7 & 5 & r3 \\ \hline 4 & {}_4 5 & {}_3 3 \end{array}$$

With 453 mushrooms in the fridge, Wallace can make 75 portions of vegetable pie with 3 mushrooms left over.

- 6 doesn't go into 4.
- 6 into 45 goes 7 times with a remainder of 3 (this 3 is carried over to the next column).
- 6 into 33 goes 5 times with a remainder of 3.

1

Use the written method to work out the answer to these questions.

a.

$$6 \begin{array}{|ccc} 8 & 5 & 2 \end{array}$$

b.

$$7 \begin{array}{|ccc} 5 & 4 & 3 \end{array}$$

c.

$$8 \begin{array}{|ccc} 5 & 6 & 7 \end{array}$$

d.

$$9 \begin{array}{|ccc} 9 & 6 & 7 \end{array}$$

2

Can you do the same for these longer numbers?

a.

$$4 \begin{array}{|cccc} 5 & 2 & 0 & 9 \end{array}$$

b.

$$8 \begin{array}{|cccc} 4 & 0 & 3 & 5 \end{array}$$

c.

$$3 \begin{array}{|cccc} 8 & 0 & 1 & 6 \end{array}$$

d.

$$7 \begin{array}{|cccc} 2 & 3 & 3 & 7 \end{array}$$

3

Use your division knowledge to work out the missing numbers in these questions.

a.

$$3 \begin{array}{|cccc} & 7 & \boxed{} & 1 & r2 \\ \hline 2 & 3 & 7 & 5 \end{array}$$

b.

$$\boxed{} \begin{array}{|cccc} 7 & 4 & 2 & r2 \\ \hline 3 & 7 & 1 & 2 \end{array}$$

c.

$$6 \begin{array}{|cccc} 4 & 2 & 5 & \\ \hline 2 & 5 & \boxed{} & 0 \end{array}$$

d.

$$9 \begin{array}{|cccc} 6 & 2 & 4 & \boxed{} \\ \hline 5 & 6 & 2 & 4 \end{array}$$

WRITTEN DIVISION

Some of the ingredients for Wallace's favourite cake come in big packs, so Gromit has to do some tricky maths to work out how to divide them for each portion and then bake and eat them.

The flour for Wallace's favourite cake comes in a pack of 1742g and he needs 13g of flour per portion. There are lots of different ways to work out how many cakes he can make with one bag of flour. Here's one example of how to do it.

$$1742 \div 13 =$$

```
        0   1   3   4
   13 | 1   7   4   2
        1   3
      ―――――――――――――
            4   4
            3   9
      ―――――――――――――
                5   2
                5   2
            ―――――――――
                    0
```

- 13 goes into 17 once (13) with 4 remaining.
- The 4 is written underneath and the 4 in the next column is brought down to make 44.
- 13 into 44 goes 3 times (39) with 5 left over.
- The 5 is written underneath and the 2 in the next column is brought down to make 52.
- 13 into 52 goes 4 times with no remainders.

1

Work out the answers to these long division questions.
The 12 times table has been shown to help you with the working out.

a.

```
12 | 1   4   7   6
```

b.

```
12 | 1   7   4   0
```

c.

```
12 | 1   8   6   0
```

d.

```
12 | 3   7   4   4
```

1 x 12 =	12
2 x 12 =	24
3 x 12 =	36
4 x 12 =	48
5 x 12 =	60
6 x 12 =	72
7 x 12 =	84
8 x 12 =	96
9 x 12 =	108
10 x 12 =	120
11 x 12 =	132
12 x 12 =	144

FRACTIONS

Wallace and Gromit like nothing better than getting a delivery of cheese! They are planning a party, so it's important that enough cheese wheels are ordered and that they are shared equally between the guests.

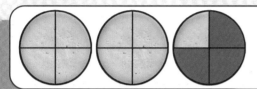

The quantity of whole cheese wheels can be written as:

$2\frac{1}{4}$ (mixed number fraction) or $\frac{9}{4}$ (improper fraction)

1

Fill in the table, writing the quantity of whole cheese wheels as a mixed number fraction and an improper fraction.

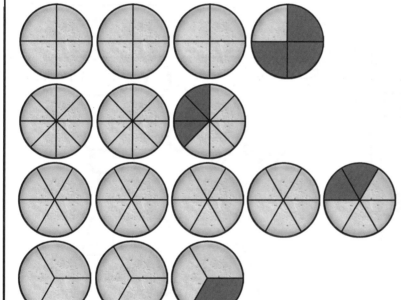

Mixed number fraction	Improper fraction

2

Write these mixed number fractions as improper fractions e.g. $2\frac{3}{5} = \frac{13}{5}$

a. $3\frac{2}{3} = \frac{\square}{\square}$

b. $2\frac{4}{7} = \frac{\square}{\square}$

c. $6\frac{1}{2} = \frac{\square}{\square}$

d. $5\frac{2}{5} = \frac{\square}{\square}$

e. $4\frac{1}{6} = \frac{\square}{\square}$

f. $7\frac{3}{4} = \frac{\square}{\square}$

3

Convert these improper fractions to mixed number fractions.

a. $\frac{8}{3} = \square\frac{\square}{\square}$

b. $\frac{17}{6} = \square\frac{\square}{\square}$

c. $\frac{17}{5} = \square\frac{\square}{\square}$

d. $\frac{19}{2} = \square\frac{\square}{\square}$

e. $\frac{21}{4} = \square\frac{\square}{\square}$

f. $\frac{22}{7} = \square\frac{\square}{\square}$

ADDING FRACTIONS

Gromit is cutting up cheese for his cheese boxes. He's recording the amounts in fractions and checking the amounts to see what they add up to.

When adding fractions, Gromit knows that if the denominator (the bottom number) of the two fractions are the same then you simply add the numerators (top numbers) together: $\frac{1}{5} + \frac{3}{5} = \frac{4}{5}$

1

Add these fractions together and write each answer as an improper fraction.

a.
$$\frac{2}{6} + \frac{5}{6} = \frac{\square}{\square}$$

b.
$$\frac{13}{10} + \frac{6}{10} = \frac{\square}{\square}$$

c.
$$\frac{3}{4} + \frac{3}{4} + \frac{1}{4} = \frac{\square}{\square}$$

d.
$$\frac{19}{8} + \frac{5}{8} + \frac{13}{8} = \frac{\square}{\square}$$

2

When the denominator is different you need to find a common multiple and make an equivalent fraction e.g. $\frac{3}{4} + \frac{2}{3}$ has a common denominator of 12 so $\frac{9}{12} + \frac{8}{12} = \frac{17}{12}$

Find a common denominator and work out these fraction sums.
Write your answers as improper fractions.

a.
$$\frac{1}{2} + \frac{2}{6} = \frac{\square}{\square}$$

b.
$$\frac{3}{5} + \frac{7}{10} = \frac{\square}{\square}$$

c.
$$\frac{1}{4} + \frac{1}{3} = \frac{\square}{\square}$$

d.
$$\frac{1}{2} + \frac{4}{5} = \frac{\square}{\square}$$

e.
$$\frac{3}{4} + \frac{3}{5} = \frac{\square}{\square}$$

f.
$$\frac{2}{3} + \frac{3}{5} = \frac{\square}{\square}$$

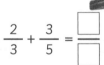

3

Complete the fraction sums and draw a circle around all the answers that would be 3 or more as a mixed number fraction.

a.
$$\frac{5}{3} + \frac{7}{6} = \boxed{}$$

b.
$$\frac{5}{2} + \frac{4}{3} = \boxed{}$$

c.
$$\frac{9}{5} + \frac{12}{10} = \boxed{}$$

d.
$$\frac{7}{5} + \frac{14}{10} = \boxed{}$$

e.
$$\frac{10}{4} + \frac{10}{5} = \boxed{}$$

f.
$$\frac{7}{3} + \frac{4}{5} = \boxed{}$$

SUBTRACTING FRACTIONS

Sometimes Gromit puts too much cheese in the boxes. He then needs to take some of the pieces out.

When subtracting fractions where the denominator (the bottom number) of the two fractions is the same, you simply subtract one numerator (top number) from the other numerator. For example: $\frac{3}{5} - \frac{1}{5} = \frac{2}{5}$

 1

Solve these subtraction questions and write your answers as improper fractions.

a.
$$\frac{17}{8} - \frac{4}{8} = \frac{\Box}{\Box}$$

b.
$$\frac{9}{2} - \frac{4}{2} = \frac{\Box}{\Box}$$

c.
$$\frac{13}{4} - \frac{5}{4} = \frac{\Box}{\Box}$$

d.
$$\frac{13}{3} - \frac{5}{3} = \frac{\Box}{\Box}$$

2

When the denominator is different, you need to find a common multiple and make an equivalent fraction e.g. $\frac{3}{4} - \frac{2}{3}$ has a common denominator of 12 so $\frac{9}{12} - \frac{8}{12} = \frac{1}{12}$.

Work out the answers to these subtraction questions and write your answers as improper fractions.

a.
$$\frac{8}{2} - \frac{5}{6} = \boxed{}$$

b.
$$\frac{10}{4} - \frac{7}{5} = \boxed{}$$

c.
$$\frac{14}{5} - \frac{4}{3} = \boxed{}$$

d.
$$\frac{6}{2} - \frac{9}{5} = \boxed{}$$

 3

Complete these number sentences and then choose the correct sign <,> or = to fill the box. The first one has been done for you.

a.
$$\frac{9}{2} - \frac{3}{2} = \frac{18}{10} - \frac{15}{10} = \frac{3}{10} < 1$$

b.
$$\frac{24}{3} - \frac{9}{2} = \frac{\Box}{\Box} - \frac{\Box}{\Box} = \frac{\Box}{\Box} \, \Box \, 3$$

c.
$$\frac{9}{2} - \frac{6}{3} = \frac{\Box}{\Box} - \frac{\Box}{\Box} = \frac{\Box}{\Box} \, \Box \, 1$$

d.
$$\frac{8}{2} - \frac{12}{5} = \frac{\Box}{\Box} - \frac{\Box}{\Box} = \frac{\Box}{\Box} \, \Box \, 2$$

e.
$$\frac{7}{3} - \frac{2}{4} = \frac{\Box}{\Box} - \frac{\Box}{\Box} = \frac{\Box}{\Box} \, \Box \, 1$$

f.
$$\frac{7}{3} - \frac{1}{5} = \frac{\Box}{\Box} - \frac{\Box}{\Box} = \frac{\Box}{\Box} \, \Box \, 2$$

MULTIPLYING FRACTIONS

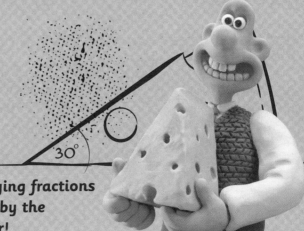

Wallace is a super inventor and thinks that multiplying fractions is easy! You simply need to multiply the numerator by the numerator and the denominator by the denominator!

For example:

$\frac{3}{5} \times \frac{1}{3}$ = (3 x 1 = 3) and (5 x 3 = 15) therefore the answer is $\frac{3}{15}$

You can then simplify the fraction:

$\frac{3}{15} = \frac{1}{5}$

At the cheese shop that Wallace goes to, they sell cheese wheels as a mix and match. Sometimes people come in with the trickiest orders! Today, someone wants to order $\frac{2}{5}$ of Stinking Bishop, $\frac{2}{5}$ of Brie and $\frac{2}{5}$ cheddar. While Wallace is waiting in the queue, he works out exactly how many whole cheese wheels the worker will make up for this order. He thinks to himself,

"What is $\frac{2}{5}$ x 3?"

1

Match the multiplying fraction number sentences with its answer in the simplest form.

a. $\frac{1}{4} \times \frac{2}{3}$ $\frac{1}{5}$

b. $\frac{3}{5} \times \frac{1}{3}$ $\frac{2}{27}$

c. $\frac{4}{8} \times \frac{2}{4}$ $\frac{1}{6}$

d. $\frac{6}{7} \times \frac{3}{5}$ $\frac{18}{35}$

e. $\frac{1}{6} \times \frac{4}{9}$ $\frac{1}{4}$

Steps to multiplying a fraction by a whole number:

- Turn the whole number into a fraction by making the denominator 1. E.g. $3 = \frac{3}{1}$
- Multiply the numerators together: 2 x 3 = 6
- Multiply the denominators together: 5 x 1 = 5
- This will give an improper fraction: $\frac{6}{5}$
- Convert the improper fraction into a mixed number fraction $\frac{6}{5} = 1\frac{1}{5}$

This means the worker will need to make 1 wheel of cheese and $\frac{1}{5}$ of a wheel for this order.

2

Fill in the missing boxes to work out how much cheese he will need to make for the following orders:

Cheese order	Calculation	How many wheels will he need to make?
$\frac{1}{2}$ Cheddar $\frac{1}{2}$ Swiss cheese	$\frac{1}{2}$ x2	
$\frac{4}{6}$ Cheddar $\frac{4}{6}$ Skinking Bishop $\frac{4}{6}$ Swiss cheese	$\frac{4}{6}$ x3	
$\frac{3}{8}$ Cheddar $\frac{3}{8}$ Brie $\frac{3}{8}$ Skinking Bishop $\frac{3}{8}$ Swiss cheese		

ORDERING FRACTIONS

SCAN CODE
purple mash

Wendolene is learning about fractions so she can work out the quantity of wool she has in her wool balls.

- A decimal is a number that is in between whole numbers and written with a dot.
- A proper fraction is a fraction that is less than one.
- An improper fraction is fraction that is greater than one.
- A mixed number fraction is written as a sum of a whole number and a fraction. For example, $1\frac{4}{5}$

1

Can you help Wendolene rewrite these fractions and decimals in order from smallest to greatest?

a. $\frac{1}{4}$ $\frac{3}{4}$ 0.5 $\frac{1}{8}$ 0.8 $\frac{7}{10}$

☐ ☐ ☐ ☐ ☐ ☐

b. $\frac{10}{12}$ $\frac{1}{9}$ 0.1 $\frac{5}{10}$ $\frac{1}{3}$ $\frac{2}{8}$

☐ ☐ ☐ ☐ ☐ ☐

c. $1\frac{1}{4}$ 0.4   0.7 $\frac{10}{5}$ $2\frac{2}{3}$ $\frac{1}{2}$

☐ ☐ ☐ ☐ ☐ ☐

d. $1\frac{3}{4}$ $\frac{7}{2}$ 0.25 $\frac{1}{8}$ 0.3 $\frac{9}{6}$

☐ ☐ ☐ ☐ ☐ ☐

2

Now colour the boxes where you have written the fractions and decimals according to the key below:

Improper fractions: colour in **red**   Mixed number fractions: colour in green

Proper fractions: colour in blue   Decimals: colour in yellow

RATIO AND PROPORTION

Preston is trying out delicious new dog food recipes. He wants to make something that no other dog has ever tried before.

He has mixed 4 green vegetables and 8 orange vegetables for recipe 1. The proportion of green vegetables is 4 out of 12. The ratio of green to orange vegetables is 4:8 simplified as 1:2.

1

Complete these:

a.

Proportion of pink fish is

___ out of ___.

The ratio of pink to white

fish is ___:___

simplified as ___:___.

b.

Proportion of yellow cheese

is ___ out of ___.

The ratio of yellow to red

cheese is ___:___.

c.

Proportion of purple biscuits

is ____ out of ____.

The ratio of purple to brown

biscuits is ___:___

simplified as ___:___.

2

Preston's favourite recipe mixture has the ratio of 3 purple biscuits to 5 brown biscuits.

Preston has decided to try out more recipes. These are the ratios he likes best.
Colour in the following to make his perfect concotions:

a. 4 green to 1 red (4:1)

b. 2 red to 5 purple (2:5)

c. 4 brown to 6 red (4:6)

22

PERCENTAGES

Wallace is shopping for spare parts for his inventions.
Good news, his favourite shop has a sale on!
Wallace needs to understand percentages to work
out how much money he will save.

'Per cent' (%) means 'out of 100'. It is a whole that has been
divided into 100 parts so, for example, 60% means 60 out of 100.

1

Help Wallace find the percentages of these numbers.

a. 50% of 100 = ☐　　**g.** 50% of 200 = ☐

b. 25% of 100 = ☐　　**h.** 25% of 200 = ☐

c. 10% of 100 = ☐　　**i.** 10% of 200 = ☐

d. 5% of 100 = ☐　　**j.** 5% of 200 = ☐

e. 30% of 100 = ☐　　**k.** 30% of 200 = ☐

f. 70% of 100 = ☐　　**l.** 70% of 200 = ☐

2

Wallace has spotted an engine with a price tag of £25 that has 10% off.
To work out the new price of the engine, Wallace first needs to work out 10% of £25: 25 ÷ 10 = 2.5, so 10% of £25 is £2.50.
Next, Wallace needs to subtract the 10% saving from the original price of the engine: 25 - 2.50 = 22.50 so the new price of the engine is £22.50.
What a bargain!

Draw lines to match each engine with the correct saving and new price.
The first one has been done for you.

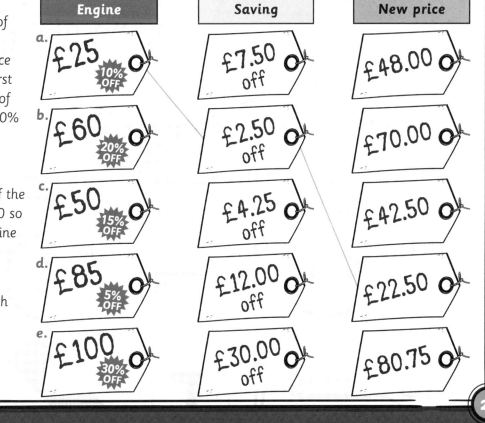

Engine	Saving	New price
a. £25 10% OFF	£7.50 off	£48.00
b. £60 20% OFF	£2.50 off	£70.00
c. £50 15% OFF	£4.25 off	£42.50
d. £85 5% OFF	£12.00 off	£22.50
e. £100 30% OFF	£30.00 off	£80.75

SCALE FACTORS

Wendolene needs to increase the size of the jumper she's making. Using complicated scientific equations, she's worked out how to increase the size of 2D objects.

The size by which she chooses to increase the jumper is called the scale factor. She starts by knitting a simple 3cm x 3cm square. To increase its size by the scale factor of 2, the measurements of each side are doubled (x 2).

3cm · 3cm

Increase: Scale factor 2 (3 x 2 = 6)

6cm · 6cm

(Not drawn to scale)

1

Here are some more shapes that Wendolene has increased. Can you work out the scale factor she used for each of the enlargements? Also, fill in the missing lengths.

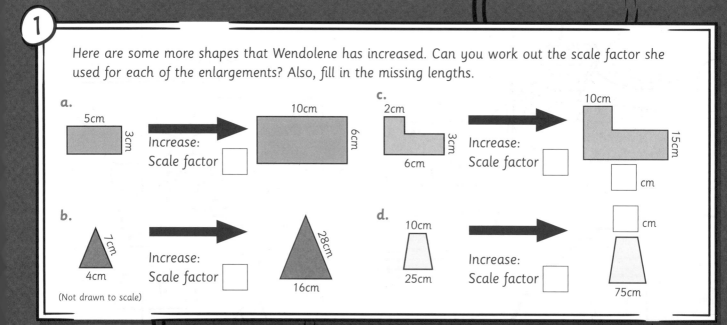

a.
5cm · 3cm
Increase: Scale factor ☐
10cm · 6cm

b.
7cm · 4cm
(Not drawn to scale)
Increase: Scale factor ☐
28cm · 16cm

c.
2cm · 3cm · 6cm
Increase: Scale factor ☐
10cm · 15cm · ☐ cm

d.
10cm · 25cm
Increase: Scale factor ☐
☐ cm · 75cm

2

Increase this triangle by the scale factor of 2. Draw the increased shape next to it.
Scale: 1 square = 1cm.

SIMPLE FORMULAE

Wallace's inventions are so loud Gromit can't concentrate on his formulas. He needs them for so many things!

1

Can you help Gromit work out the value of the letters? The first one has been done for you.

a. $x + 5 = 9$

$x = \boxed{4}$

b. $y + 7 = 22$

$y = \boxed{}$

c. $n - 6 = 9$

$n = \boxed{}$

d. $x - 7 = 3$

$x = $

e. $7y = 35$

$y = $

f. $\dfrac{x}{6} = 6$

$x = $

2

Now try these trickier formulae. The first one has been done for you.

a. $3x + 4 = 10$

$3x = \boxed{6}$

$x = \boxed{2}$

b. $6a + 5 = 29$

$6a = \boxed{}$

$a = \boxed{}$

c. $3n - 2 = 25$

$3n = \boxed{}$

$n = \boxed{}$

d. $2 + 8c = 26$

$8c = \boxed{}$

$c = \boxed{}$

e. $\dfrac{n}{9} + 4 = 9$

$\dfrac{n}{9} = \boxed{}$

$n = \boxed{}$

f. $12 - x = 2$

$x = \boxed{}$

g. $7c + 12 = 47$

$7c = \boxed{}$

$c = \boxed{}$

h. $9 + 6a = 57$

$6a = \boxed{}$

$a = \boxed{}$

i. $43 - 4n = 23$

$4n = \boxed{}$

$n = \boxed{}$

NUMBER SEQUENCES

Wallace is building a rocket. He's created a schedule of what he has to do each day. Can you work out how many times he needs to repeat each exercise each day by using the rule to complete the sequence?

1

Rule	Monday	Tuesday	Wednesday	Thursday	Friday	Saturday	Sunday
Paint the rocket (add 6)	2	8	14	20	26	32	38
Prepare crackers (double)	1 minute						
Build the ladder (subtract 7)	42 minutes						
Pack (double and add 1)	2						
Check the electronics (multiply by 3 then add 2)	2						
Work on the roof opening (add 4 and double)	2						
Rest (halve and subtract 5)	10 minutes 30 seconds (Tip: convert this to seconds first = 630 seconds)						

ALGEBRA WORD PROBLEMS

Wallace and Gromit have some tricky calculations to solve when looking at their calendar. Use your algebra skills to help them work out the answers.

1

Gromit is trying to work out how many days it is until Fluffles' birthday. They know that it is 8 weeks and then 3 more days.

a. Can you write a formula to calculate the number of days until Fluffles' birthday, where the letter d stands for 'days until birthday' and the letter w stands for 'number of weeks'?

b. Use the formula to work out the number of days until Fluffles' birthday.

2

Gromit is trying to work out whether he has enough money for fancy gift wrapping for Fluffles' present. Bows cost 12p. Wrapping paper cost 25p.

a. Write an equation to work out the total cost, using b for bows, s for wrapping paper and c for the total cost.

b. He has 75p. Can he afford two pieces of wrapping paper and two bows?

c. Wallace gives him another 45p. How much does he have altogether now?

d. If he buys three bows, how many pieces of wrapping paper can he afford?

3

Wallace is having a sale at his bakery. How much should he charge for his bread? He wants to make £18.20.

a. Write a formula that calculates how much he needs to charge for each loaf in pence (t) if p is the number of people who buy a loaf, in order to raise the total amount.

b. He thinks that 13 people will buy a loaf. How much should he charge in pounds and pence?

4

Wallace gave half his loaves to the village fair, then made 3 more loaves in his bakery. Now he has 12 loaves. Write a formula to calculate the number of loaves that he started with (p) and solve the equation.

CONVERTING UNITS OF MEASUREMENT

SCAN CODE

Wallace and Wendolene usually get on well together but for some reason, they are disagreeing about absolutely everything today. Use this conversion table to help you work out who is right.

Capacity
1 litre (l) = 1000 millilitres (ml)
1 centilitre (cl) = 10ml

Mass
1 kilogram (kg) = 1000 grams (g)
1 tonne = 1000kg

Length
1 centimetre (cm) = 10 millimetres (mm)
1 metre (m) = 100cm
1 kilometre (km) = 1000m

1

Wallace has a ball of wool that is 5.6m and another that is 650mm.

Tick who has more.

Wendolene has 6 whole metres of wool.

2

It is 4.6km drive to the supermarket and then a 250m walk. Wallace wants to go there.

Tick who is right.

Wendolene thinks that the village store is much nearer, it is just 3.2km and a 535m walk.

3

Wallace has a bottle of window wash. It has 5325ml.

Tick who has the best value.

Wendolene has a bottle of Suds-U-Like. There are 0.25l in each can and there are 30 bottles for the same price.

4

Wallace has a huge bag of tea bags, it weighs half a kg.

Wendolene has a multipack, there are 6 packs of 80g for the same price.

Which should they buy?

5

Circle the values that are equivalent in each row.

a	35cm	350cl	350mm	3.5cm	3.5m	0.35m
b	0.4kg	400g	40g	400ml	4kg	4g
c	14cl	1.4kg	140g	140ml	0.14l	0.014l
d	1560kg	1560g	15.6 tonnes	1.56 tonnes	15600g	1560000g

PERIMETER

Never one to rest on his laurels, Wallace is helping his neighbour build some new garden fences. He has to calculate the gardens' perimeters to work out how many fence panels his new fence-building invention will need.

Perimeter is the distance around the edges of the shape.

In the example this is 7cm + 3cm + 7cm + 3cm = 20cm

7m

3m

1

Calculate the perimeters for these gardens. 1 square = 1m.

a.
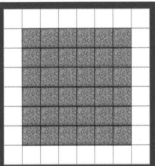

b.
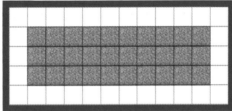

c.
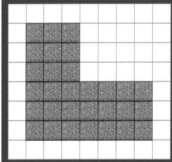

d.
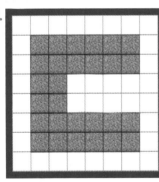

e.
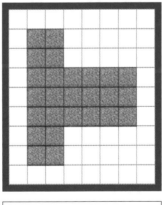

f.
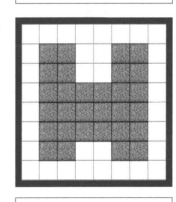

g.
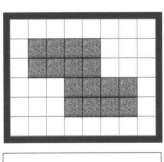

h.
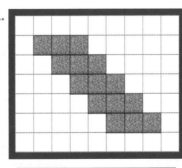

i.
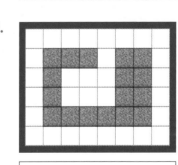

CALCULATING AREA

His neighbour also wants to grow grass in their garden. Wallace needs to work out the area of their garden so he can buy the right amount of grass seed. After a cup of tea of course.

1

Look at the gardens on the previous page and calculate the area for each garden.

Remember that area is calculated as square units, in this case square metres or m². Split the gardens into rectangle shapes and then calculate the area of each part by multiplying the width by the length.

a.	b.	c.
d.	e.	f.
g.	h.	i.

2

Wallace is moving his basement around to make room for his new invention. Look at the plan and calculate the area of the different objects in square metres.

Hint: Remember, to work out the area of a triangle, you multiply the height by the width (also known as the base), then divide by 2.

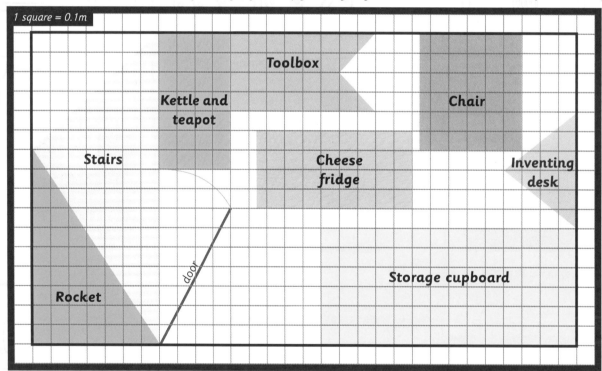

1 square = 0.1m

Toolbox

Kettle and teapot

Chair

Stairs

Cheese fridge

Inventing desk

door

Storage cupboard

Rocket

a. **Storage cupboard** =

b. **Inventing desk** =

c. **Kettle and teapot** =

d. **Stairs** =

e. **Cheese fridge** =

f. **Rocket** =

g. **Chair** =

h. **Toolbox** =

CALCULATING AREA

Feathers McGraw is working out his plans to steal the blue diamond from the museum. Although the two rectangular rooms in the museum are different lengths and widths, they both have a perimeter of 72m.

1

Work out how many possible widths and lengths the areas could be, if both have widths and lengths in whole numbers of metres.

2

Can you write a rule that applies to working out any perimeter?

3

Even though the two rooms have the same perimeter, they have different areas.

a. What is the width and length that would make the maximum possible area?

b. What is the maximum possible area?

4

Feathers has worked out the two rooms have a difference of 57m2.

Work out the possible widths and lengths of the rooms.

Hint: Use what you know about the possible lengths and widths to work out all of the possible areas until you find two that have a difference in area of 57m².

MILES AND KILOMETRES

Determined to show off his football skills, Wallace and Gromit are taking it in turns to use the Soccamatic to kick dozens of balls as far as possible. The pair have worked out the distances the balls travelled using a map.

They know that 1 mile = 1.6km.

1

Work out these distances in km.

Miles	1	5	4.5	9	12.5
Km					

2

Work out these distances in miles.

Miles					
Km	11.2	10.4	9.6	16	5.6

3

Whose ball has travelled furthest? Use the <, > and = signs to complete these number sentences.

Wallce	<, > or =	Gromit
3 miles		4km
3.5 miles		5.6km
5.5 miles		8km
8 miles		13km
11.5 miles		18.4km

ANGLES

Wallace and Gromit are trying out the Porridge Gun so breakfast can go with a bang. Gromit is using his knowledge of angles to make sure he hits the right target every time.

When two lines meet at a shared point, it creates an angle. The bigger the space between the two lines, the bigger the angle. The size of an angle is measures in degrees (°).
There are four types of angles that you need to remember:

Right angle	Acute angle	Obtuse angle	Reflex angle
A right angle is exactly 90°. A square is made up of 4 right angles.	An acute angle is any angle which is smaller than 90°.	An obtuse angle is any angle between 90° and 180°.	A reflex angle is any angle between 180° and 360°.

1

Look at the different angles below. Underneath each one, write down whether it is a right, acute, obtuse or reflex angle.

a. [ ] b. [ ] c. [ ] d. [ ] e. [ ]

2

Look at the marked angles on the shapes below. Use the colour key to shade the angles the correct colour.

Obtuse [ ]   Acute [ ]   Right [ ]   Reflex [ ]

a.   b.   c.   d.   e.

MISSING ANGLES

SCAN CODE
purple mash

Gromit wants to work out the perfect angle to fire the porridge from the gun. First, he needs to study the rules below which will help him work out the angles.

Angles on a straight line always add up to 180°.	The three internal angles of a triangle always add up to 180°.	Angles around a point always add up to 360°.	When two straight lines cross each other, the angles opposite each other are the same.
130° / 50°	45° / 90° / 45°	240° / 120°	100° / 80° / 80° / 100°

(Angles not to scale)

1

Write the missing angles in the boxes below.

a.

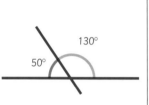

60° | ☐°

b.

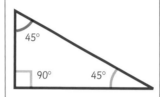

☐° / 55° / 82°

c.

116° / ☐°

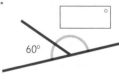

d.

70° / ☐° / 32°

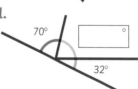

e.

125° / ☐° / ☐°

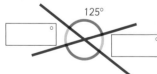

f.

53° / ☐°

g.

133° / ☐° / ☐° / 30°

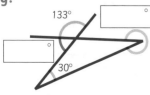

h.

☐° / ☐° / 81° / 107°

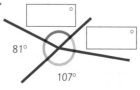

(Angles not to scale)

2

Four angles meet together at a point.

One of the angles is a right angle.

One of the angles is 68°.

The two unknown angles are equal.

How many degrees are each of the unknown angles?

Draw a rough diagram of the angles to prove your answer.

PROBABILITY

Wallace wants to calculate the probability of which baked items are most likely to sell by the end of the day.

Probability, which means the likelihood of something happening, can be expressed on a scale ranging from impossible to certain.

It is almost certain that Wallace will have cheese with his crackers.

1

For each question, look at the pictures of the selection available and circle how likely the event is to happen.

a.
Select a loaf

| Impossible | Unlikely | Even chance | Likely | Certain |

b.
Select a bloomer

| Impossible | Unlikely | Even chance | Likely | Certain |

c.
Select a cottage loaf

| Impossible | Unlikely | Even chance | Likely | Certain |

d.
Select a roll

| Impossible | Unlikely | Even chance | Likely | Certain |

e.
Select an iced bun

| Impossible | Unlikely | Even chance | Likely | Certain |

PROBABILITY

As well as being measured on a scale, probability (the likelihood of something happening), can be measured using fractions, decimals and percentages.

1

Wallace and Gromit are playing a game using a spinner with numbers from 1 to 10 stuck onto a wheel of cheese. Can you work out how likely they are to land on the numbers described opposite and draw lines to the correct answers? The first one has been done for you.

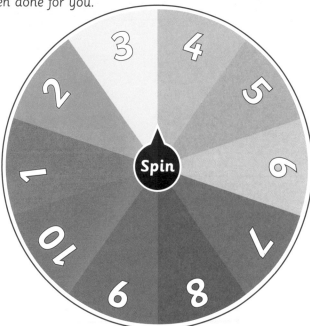

a. A nine — $\dfrac{1}{2}$

b. A red or yellow number — $\dfrac{1}{10}$

c. A number divisible by three — 0.3

d. A number greater than 5 — 40%

e. A number less than 5 — 20%

f. A number greater than 3 — 0.7

2

As a percentage, what is the probability that Gromit will spin a 1, 5 or 7?

3

As a fraction, what is the probability that Wallace will spin a number divisible by 4?

4

As a decimal, what is the probability that Gromit will spin an even number?

COORDINATES

Wallace and Gromit have taken a trip to the moon in the hope of finding the best cheese and have taken a picnic with them.

1

The black dots show the locations of Wallace and Gromit, the rocket and its contents. Can you fill in the coordinates of each location? The first has been completed for you. Use the last, empty space to add yourself to the grid and write the coordinates for your own location.

Remember, when you write and read coordinates, you take the x axis first and then the y axis.

So (3,5) means three across and then five up.

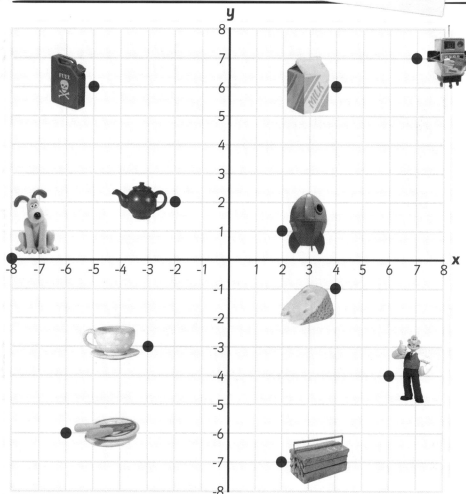

a. Teapot (-2, 2)   b. Wallace (☐ , ☐)   c. Gromit (☐ , ☐)

d. Cooker (☐ , ☐)   e. Rocket (☐ , ☐)   f. Tool box  (☐ , ☐)

g. Cheese (☐ , ☐)   h. Fuel can (☐ , ☐)   i. Picnic dishes (☐ , ☐)

j. Tea cup  (☐ , ☐)   k. Milk carton (☐ , ☐)   l. _____ (☐ , ☐)

COORDINATES

Wallace has had to chase off after Gromit and has got lost in the woods. Use the given coordinates to track down Gromit's locations.

a. (1, 2)   Where was Gromit seen?

b. (4, 7)   Where was Gromit seen?

c. (0, -5)   Where was Gromit seen?

d. (6, 1)   Where was Gromit seen?

TRANSLATION

Feathers McGraw has selected a few favourite items that he'd like to steal from the museum. He's using translation to work out how to get the items out of the museum.

A translation is a type of transformation. It moves a shape up, down or from left to right, but it does not change its appearance in any other way.

1

Complete the sentences by filling in the gaps and crossing out the incorrect choices to show the translation Feathers has used to go from shape a to b.

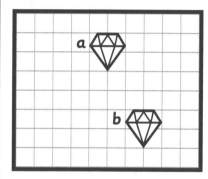 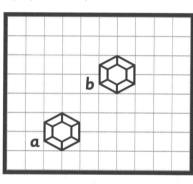 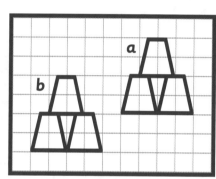

a. The diamond has been translated ☐ squares to the left/right and ☐ squares up/down.

b. The ruby has been translated ☐ squares left/right and ☐ squares up/down.

c. The gold has been translated ☐ squares left/right and ☐ squares up/down.

2

Complete the pattern by redrawing the shapes according to Feather's instructions.

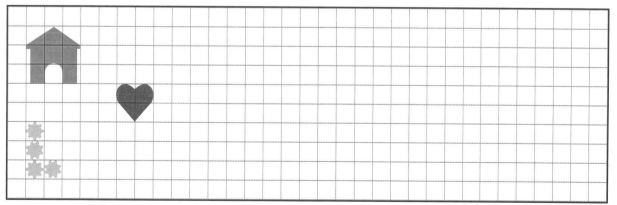

Translate the shapes as follows:

a. Translate the cogs 10 squares to the right and 3 squares up.

b. Translate the heart 3 squares to the right and 2 squares up.

c. Translate the dog house 6 squares to the right and 5 squares down.

REFLECTION

Piella has a favourite mirror that she uses every day. She has been thinking about reflection, which is a type of transformation.

When an object is reflected, it needs a mirror line. The object's size doesn't change, the image just appears flipped so that every point on the shape is the same distance away on the other side of the mirror line.

1

Reflect the letters of Piella's name in the mirror lines. The first one has been done for you.

2

Can you shade the right side of Gromit so that it's a reflection of his left side?

3

Look at the images of Fluffles below. Can you work out which are translations, which are reflections and which are neither?

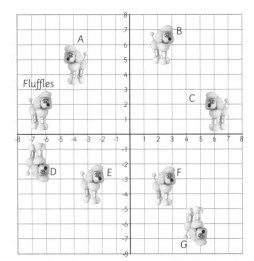

a. Translations:

c. Neither translations or reflections:

b. Reflections:

LINE GRAPHS

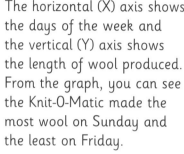

Wallace has been using the Knit-O-Matic and has created line graphs to keep track of its knitting.

How much wool in a week

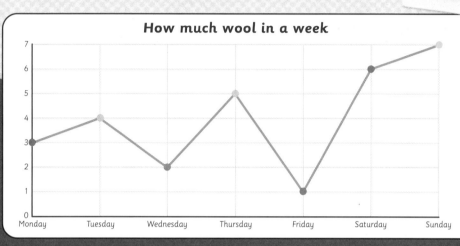

The horizontal (X) axis shows the days of the week and the vertical (Y) axis shows the length of wool produced. From the graph, you can see the Knit-O-Matic made the most wool on Sunday and the least on Friday.

1

Number of washed sheep

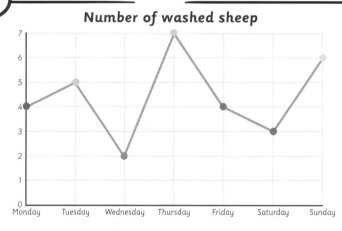

Wallace has been washing sheep by hand to try and keep up with the Knit-O-Matic. This line graph shows the number of sheep Wallace has washed.

Look at the graph and use it to answer these questions.

a. On what day did he wash the greatest number of sheep?

b. On what day did he wash the least number of sheep?

c. On what days did he wash 4 sheep?

2

Wallace vs Knit-0-Matic

— Wallace
— Knit-O-Matic

This line graph shows the number of sheep Wallace and the Knit-O-Matic washed over 10 weeks. Fill in the table below to work out who's scored the most and is the winner.

The winner is _____.

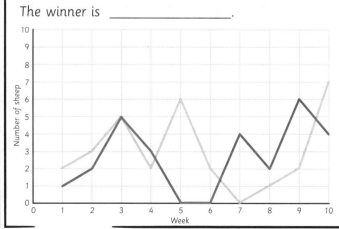

Week	Sheep - Wallace	Sheep – Knit-O-Matic
1	2	1
2		
3		
4		
5		
6		
7		
8		
9		
10		

TIMETABLES

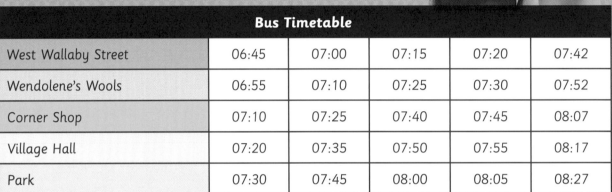

It's all go "Up North". The bus company has just updated its bus timetable. Take a look at the timetable below and answer the questions.

Bus Timetable					
West Wallaby Street	06:45	07:00	07:15	07:20	07:42
Wendolene's Wools	06:55	07:10	07:25	07:30	07:52
Corner Shop	07:10	07:25	07:40	07:45	08:07
Village Hall	07:20	07:35	07:50	07:55	08:17
Park	07:30	07:45	08:00	08:05	08:27

1

a. How long is the journey time in minutes from West Wallaby Street to the Corner Shop?

b. If Wallace arrived at the park at 07:45 and got on the bus at Wendolene's Wools, how long was he on the bus for?

c. What time does Wallace need to be at the Corner Shop if he wants to get to the park for 08:00?

d. How many minutes later is the next bus from Wendolene's Wools after 07:20?

e. Wallace says the longest time between stops is between Wendolene's Wools and the Corner Shop. True or false?

f. Wendolene says that if she boards the bus at 07:30 from Wendolene's Wools, she will get home at 08:27. True or false?

2

The return bus timetable is also being updated but it hasn't been finished yet. Can you complete it, using the timings from the first timetable to help you?

Bus Timetable					
Park	14:55	15:00	15:10	15:20	
Village Hall	15:05	15:10			15:45
Corner Shop		15:20	15:30	15:40	15:55
Wendolene's Wools	15:30	15:35	15:45		16:10
West Wallaby Street	15:40		15:55	16:05	

TIMETABLES

Look at the timetable Wallace created for giving thought to ideas for new inventions and answer the following questions.

1

Look at the timetable and answer the following questions.

	08:45 – 09:30	09:30 – 10:15	Tea break (10:15 – 10:45)	10:45 – 11:45	Lunch (11:45 – 12:45)	12:45 – 13:45	13:45 – 14:45
Monday	Loaf-counter	Memory-helper		Sleep-helper		Chores-doer	Movement-maker
Tuesday	Sleep-helper	Movement-maker		Loaf-counter		Finds things	
Wednesday	Loaf-counter	Memory-helper		Sleep-helper		Clothes-sorter	Music-machine
Thursday	Sleep-helper	Clothes-sorter		Loaf-counter		Fun-creator	
Friday	Loaf-counter	Music-machine		Sleep-helper		Memory-helper	Fixes things

a. How many times a week will Wallace brainstorm ideas for a loaf-counting invention?

b. How many hours will Wallace think about how to make a fun-creator invention on a Thursday?

c. Which days will Wallace brainstorm a sleep-helper invention after a tea break?

d. How many minutes are there of tea break each day?

2

Wallace has forgotten to add in cheese-eating to his brainstorming timetable.
To fit it in, memory-helper inventing needs to be moved. Use the information below to fill in the gaps on the timetable for cheese-eating and memory-helper inventing.

	08:45 – 09:30	09:30 – 10:15	Tea break (10:15 – 10:45)	10:45 – 11:45	Lunch (11:45 – 12:45)	12:45 – 13:45	13:45 – 14:45
Monday	Loaf-counter			Sleep-helper		Chores-doer	
Tuesday	Sleep-helper	Movement-maker		Loaf-counter		Finds things	
Wednesday	Loaf-counter	Clothes-sorter		Sleep-helper		Clothes-sorter	Music-machine
Thursday	Sleep-helper			Loaf-counter			
Friday	Loaf-counter	Music-machine		Sleep-helper			Fixes things

Cheese eating can only take place on a Monday, Thursday and Friday. There is too much of a good thing! There can be no more than one session of cheese eating in an afternoon per a week.
Memory-helper inventing must be thought about on a Monday and Thursday. Memory-helper inventing must be for an hour on a Monday. Overall, there should be 3 hours of memory-helper inventing.

PIE CHARTS

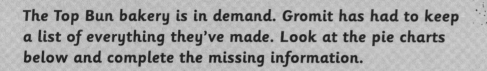

The Top Bun bakery is in demand. Gromit has had to keep a list of everything they've made. Look at the pie charts below and complete the missing information.

1 White loaves

■ Sold ■ Didn't sell ■ Burnt

Wallace and Gromit made a total of 40 white loaves.

Sold = 10   Didn't sell = ☐   Burnt = ☐

2 Baguettes

■ Sold ■ Didn't sell ■ Burnt

Wallace and Total made a total of 36 baguettes.

Sold = ☐   Didn't sell = 6   Burnt = ☐

3 Iced buns

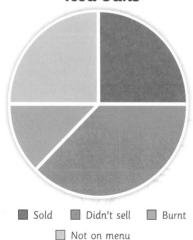

■ Sold ■ Didn't sell ■ Burnt
■ Not on menu

There were a total of 96 days when buns could have been made.

Sold = 24   Didn't sell = ☐   Burnt = 12

Not on menu = ☐

4 Birthday cakes

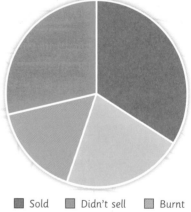

■ Sold ■ Didn't sell ■ Burnt
■ Not on menu

There were a total of 112 birthday days when cakes could have been made.

Sold = ☐   Didn't sell = 24   Burnt = 18

Not on menu = 26